The Darkness of Faith

'Enfolded in love' series
General Editor: Robert Llewelyn

ENFOLDED IN LOVE *(Julian of Norwich)*
Robert Llewelyn

IN LOVE ENCLOSED *(Julian of Norwich)*
Robert Llewelyn

THE DART OF LONGING LOVE
('The Cloud of Unknowing')
Robert Llewelyn

AN ORATORY OF THE HEART
(Brother Lawrence)
Robert Llewelyn

THE FLAME OF DIVINE LOVE
(Jean-Pierre de Caussade)
Robert Llewelyn

ATHIRST FOR GOD *(St Francis de Sales)*
Michael Hollings

BY LOVE ALONE *(St Thérèse of Lisieux)*
Michael Hollings

FIRE FROM A FLINT *(William Law)*
Robert Llewelyn and Edward Moss

THE GIFT OF LOVE *(John Wesley)*
Arthur Skevington Wood

THE HEART AT REST *(St Augustine)*
Dame Maura Sée OSB

LAMPS OF FIRE *(St John of the Cross)*
Sister Elizabeth Ruth ODC

LIVING WATER *(St Teresa of Avila)*
Sister Mary ODC

THRESHOLD OF LIGHT *(The Celtic Tradition)*
A. M. Allchin and Esther de Waal

THE DARKNESS OF FAITH

Daily Readings with
Martin Luther

Introduced and edited by
James Atkinson

Darton, Longman and Todd
London

First published in 1987 by
Darton, Longman and Todd Ltd
89 Lillie Road, London SW6 1UD

Introduction, translation and arrangement
© 1987 James Atkinson

ISBN 0 232 51700 2

242 2

British Library Cataloguing in Publication Data

Luther, Martin, *1483–1546*
    The darkness of faith: daily readings
    with Martin Luther.—(Enfolded in love
    series)
    1. Devotional calendars
    I. Title II. Atkinson, James, *1914–*
    III. Series
    242'.2   BV4810

    ISBN 0–232–51700–2

Phototypeset by
Input Typesetting Ltd, London SW19 8DR
Printed and bound in Great Britain by
Anchor Brendon Ltd, Tiptree, Essex

Contents

Martin Luther: his spiritual pilgrimage

Martin Luther: his spiritual pilgrimage

Luther's sole concern was to preach Christ: no other achievement takes precedence, no other activity should be allowed to obscure this. In fact, all that Luther said and did subsumes this single overriding concern. As he wrote in his Preface to his Lectures on Galatians,

> For the one doctrine which I have supremely at heart is that of faith in Christ, from whom, through whom and unto whom all my theological thinking flows back and forth day and night.

He summarized St Paul's work with words he could have made his own:

> As if he meant to say, I have taught you Christ, purely and simply, as He is.

Here one touches the heartbeat of Luther. To learn this is to learn all of Luther. This was Luther's God-given mission: to preach Christ.

He was born on 10 November 1483, of Hans and Margaret Luther, in Eisleben, Saxony. Both parents were deeply religious, and the young Martin grew up in a godly home strongly supported by upright, independently minded, hardworking parents. His parents gave the bright boy a first-class education: Martin went to school with the privileged boys of the neighbourhood, and, at his father's expense, eventually was sent to the University of Erfurt, one of Germany's oldest and most prestigious universities.

LUTHER INCOGNITO
(in safe custody at the impregnable castle The
Wartburg, masquerading as 'Sir George', 1521–22)
Credit: Mansell Collection

He was noticed at school and at church for his deep attentiveness in matters religious, and fulfilled these promising beginnings at the university. At the completion of his studies he had a terrifying experience of death. It was death which brought Luther face to face with the meaning of life. He realized that he was not able to make the journey through death, and vowed to become a monk to fit himself to face God. He entered the monastery of the Augustinian Eremites at Erfurt at the age of twenty-two.

Luther made this decision because he was anxious about his soul, but was to find that the monastic discipline served not to settle his anxieties but to sharpen them. He could never feel certain that he had actually confessed all his sins, nor that he had done all that was required of him. We see in the young Luther a devout and devoted monk wrestling with God. His wise preceptor, sensibly, refused to listen to his multitudinous confessions, or to his self-concern for his soul's health. He reassured Luther of God's continuing mercy and forgiveness, pointing out that it was not the case that God was angry with Luther, but rather, that Luther was angry with God. True as these assurances were, and are, they helped Luther little, for they did not diagnose his essential conflict. Luther was right in believing that he could never know all his sin, and therefore could never know the experience of forgiveness, but only the wrath of a holy, righteous God meeting his sin. Luther was also right in believing that he could never be sure that he had done 'all that in him lay', and therefore, in spite of all spiritual discipline, could but earn God's condemnation. It was not that he was a bad and faithless monk, but that he was simply too good, too faithful, too conscientious.

As long as Luther remained within the lines of current Catholic practice, he could never break through. 'If ever a monk could have got to heaven by monkery, it would have been me!' he cried. He was later to regard the then monastic way as essentially a form of Judaism lacking the liberation the gospel effected, in that both Judaism and contemporary Catholicism were, in different degrees, a salvation by works and ethics, though, of course, both taught the primacy of grace. His spiritual problem remained essentially undiagnosed. He eventually realized that there are no 'ladders to heaven', and that the three known ladders – of intellect, of works, of mysticism – attain not God, but a concept of one's own fabrication, not the God and Father of our Lord Jesus Christ. He broke through this problem neither in the confessional, nor even at the altar, but in his study, where he eventually realized that it was by grace he was saved, not of himself: it was a gift of God. At the early stage Luther was experiencing the intense pain and anguish of half-belief and uncertainty.

Luther was not allowed to work in silence for the perfection of his soul, but was ordered to resume academic studies. His preceptors saw that he was a born teacher, a born preacher. He resumed the study of scholastic theology eagerly. He found that the scholastic theologians treated the very problems which were then besetting his mind: for example, whether a person can achieve the perfect love of God and earn the grace of God; whether sins are actually done away with in absolution; whether the will is free to do what is right; whether a soul is elected and predestined to salvation. Luther found no compelling answer in the prevalent theology of his day. To his credit, he would not allow his mind to be persuaded against his own experience. He held on to his doubt and persisted with his questions until God broke through his questions with answers, through his perplexity with certainty.

In 1508 he was called to the Chair of the new University of Wittenberg, and after an intermediate period at Erfurt, occupied the Chair until his death in 1546. At this stage he still carried his problems with him, but was considerably helped by Staupitz, his vicar-general, who had steered him into the Chair. Staupitz, a deeply spiritual man and a master in scholastic philosophy, had also an exceptional knowledge of the Bible. He argued that no man, by virtue of his own reason and strength, could ever will, know or do good. He believed that if a man was called of God and received grace through the sacraments, then the ability to will, know and do good was granted him. He admitted that no man could be certain of his election, but rather, that the sacraments nourished that hope continuously and drove out despair. He begged Luther to turn from his torments into seeking peace with God, not on the strength of his own resolutions (which he could never really carry out), nor by his own good works (which could never fully satisfy the Law of

God), but to rely solely and simply on God's forgiving mercy. He turned Luther's mind away from penance to penitence, to inward change, conversion, away from his own self-concern to the reality of God's work and God's concern for man. He taught him to think of God in terms of Christ, whom God sent not as a condemning Judge but as Saviour.

Luther's work on the Bible clarified his mind. It was after his study of the Psalms and then of Romans that he began to realize that Paul was arguing that a man was set right with God freely by grace in Christ, in other words, justified by faith, without prior works and efforts. It was the forgiving righteousness of God which set a person in a new relationship by setting him 'in Christ', not because of man's moral worth (good in itself), nor because of his works (equally good in themselves), but because it was of God's nature to have mercy and to forgive. The righteousness of God was the kind which reconciled man to himself while yet a sinner. Such righteousness was of a kind no human mind could conceive; it was a righteousness of love and mercy reaching out for a lost soul who could never on his own find God, nor ever know forgiveness. Luther discovered that

> His mercy is my justification. When I had realized this, I felt myself absolutely born again. The gates of paradise had been flung open and I had entered. There and then the whole of Scripture took on another look to me.*

* Introduction to the Latin edition of Luther's Works, 1545 (WA LIV.186).

He came painfully to realize that for over a thousand years the Church had been growing farther and farther away from the gospel. In allowing accretions and the growth of corruptions, and permitting itself to become as secularized and worldly as any prince's court, the Church had all but lost the gospel, to the despair of many saints and scholars as well as ordinary people. All that Luther did was to restore the gospel to man, and offer Christ. The corruptions and accretions simply fell away, like a scab when the wound has healed. He innovated nothing but renovated everything. He joined hands over the centuries with Athanasius and Augustine. He offered *re*formation to what had suffered *de*formation.

Perhaps Luther's pilgrimage is, *mutatis mutandis*, that of Everyman? The natural man always thinks that by his thinking, by high morality and goodness, and by prayer and spiritual discipline (all good in themselves), he can attain to God. The truth is contrary. It is only when a man realizes that he is alienated from God both in mind and soul, that he is nothing, has nothing and can do nothing which will bridge that gap and destroy that alienation, that God can ever warm his soul and enlighten his mind. In other words, he can have a right relationship to God only when he realizes that God alone can restore his mind and God alone redeem his soul. This is the meaning of justification by faith alone, or, expressed in other words, justification in Christ alone, or by grace alone. all mean the same thing. This was Luther's discovery. 'By grace are you saved, through faith; and that, not of yourselves; it is the gift of God' (Ephesians 2:8).

The next four years were formative for Luther. From 1513 to 1517 we find him forging his evangelical insights on the anvil of scholasticism. His study of the Bible opened up to him the powerful reality of the word of God, by which he meant what God was saying to the penitent and believing heart, as he read the Scriptures. The call to the Chair at Wittenberg by Staupitz constituted also a call to the pulpit, and we now see Luther expounding the Bible book by book in the university and preaching the living word from the pulpit. In 1517, he engaged on a *Disputation against Scholastic Theology* and a result of this debate was the collapse of the study of scholastic theology in Wittenberg and the rise of the study of the Bible and of Augustine. This debate was the real beginning of the Reformation, rather than the negative though better known debate on the abuse of indulgences, to which we now turn.

The castle church in Wittenberg was renowned for its unique collection of relics, 5,005 in all. Among these, it was claimed, were pieces of the burning bush of Moses, nine thorns from Jesus' crown of thorns, thirty-five fragments of the cross of Christ, some hay and straw from Christ's manger. There were remnants of the manger, the cradle and the swaddling-clothes of Christ; hair from the Blessed Virgin, phials of her milk, fragments of her petticoat and other garments; 204 pieces of the bodies of the innocent babes of Bethlehem whom Herod slew, including one body intact. It was not the singularity of the relics which was important, but their alleged spiritual potency. By adoring them, reciting the appropriate formula of prayer and paying the fee, it was computed that 127,709 years and 116 days remission of time in purgatory could be secured. This indulgence also carried with it the Portiuncula Indulgence of 1398 which further promised 'remission of punishment and guilt for all repented sins'.

The world knows the vulgar and corrupt opportunism with which the Dominican Tetzel peddled his wares.

> The dead cry, 'Pity us! Pity us! We are in dire torment from which you can redeem us for a mere pittance . . . Will you leave us here in flames? Will you delay our promised glory?'
>
> As soon as the coin in the coffer rings
> The soul from purgatory springs.
>
> Will you not then for a mere quarter of a florin receive these letters of indulgence through which you are able to lead a divine and immortal soul into the fatherland of paradise?

He claimed written authority of the pope himself of his powers 'to shut the gates of hell and open the doors of paradise'.

Luther had earlier (1515) shown a pastoral concern in this matter, and in 1517 he chose the traditional course of an academic disputation to air the whole idea. He posted up ninety-five theses, beginning with the true nature of repentance as taught by Christ and ending with an appeal for faith in Christ, not in the false assurances of indulgences.

The theses spread throughout Europe like wildfire. He was banned by the pope. He responded robustly by writing a book entitled *Explanations*, which explained for the layman the issues involved. He gave a magnificent scholarly and spiritual defence and explanation of his theology, free from conflict and polemics, before his brother monks at their triennial chapter in Heidelberg (1518). He was summoned before Cardinal Cajetan, a scholarly and uncorrupt cleric, to face a criticism of his theology and of his conduct, but returned a spirited defence (1518). He faced a lengthy disputation before the redoubtable debater John Eck, a brilliant scholar in his own right, who accused Luther of reviving heresy already condemned by council (1519). On his return to Wittenberg he realized that the Refor-

LUTHER UNDER EXAMINATION BY CARDINAL CAJETAN
(Augsburg, October 1518)

LUTHER IN ACADEMIC DISPUTATION
(with Dr Eck, Leipzig, June 1519)

mation was now under way, and that his role in
life would be to lead it. In the next year he wrote
his well-known *Reformation Writings*, *To the
German Nobility*, *The Babylonian Captivity of the
Church* and *The Freedom of the Christian* (1520), as
well as significant books on *Good Works* and on
The New Testament, that is, the Mass, and the
Papacy.

When the bill of excommunication was promulgated in 1520, Luther publicly burnt it and for
good measure threw in the Canon Law, a few
tomes of scholastic theology and some polemical
writings of an anti-evangelical kind, but only after
he had written a vigorous manifesto against the
bull. A thrill went through Europe when it learned
that an obscure monk, with no more behind him
than his faith in God, had publicly burnt a papal

bull. It was the fiery signal of emancipation of both Church and university. The individual soul had discovered its value in its courageous resistance against authority unlawfully exercised.

Every schoolchild knows of the still more courageous stand before the emperor at the Diet of Worms, April 1521, when Luther refused to recant, saying that unless he were proved wrong on the basis of the Scriptures and sound reason, for popes and councils had erred and might err again, he was fast bound by his conscience to the word of God. 'I cannot and will not recant! I can no other! Here I stand! May God help me! Amen!'

The next day he was officially informed that the emperor intended to prosecute him, but he was given a safe conduct home to Wittenberg and commanded neither to preach nor teach on the

LUTHER'S PRELIMINARY HEARING
(before the Emperor, Worms, 1521)

LUTHER'S FULL HEARING
(before the Emperor, Worms, 1521. Note the words,
'Here I stand!' written on the floor at Luther's feet!)

way. He was taken out of all the action when, on
his return journey, he was seized and locked up
in safe and friendly captivity in the Wartburg
castle. Here within a matter of a few weeks he
translated the entire New Testament into exquisite
German, and wrote many books, as well as
answering his critics.

Nevertheless, Wittenberg needed Luther, for
the movement had gone radical, negative and
destructive in his absence. He returned in 1522
and settled all this extremism, which had been
fomented and led by another and older professor,
Carlstadt. Luther was now to face all the problems
of the Reformation and indeed of his life. He had
answered the Catholic attack of Latomus of
Louvain while still at the Wartburg, but that was
to continue through Henry VIII and countless

other Catholic polemicists, most of whom were abusive and reactionary. There was also the attack of Erasmus in 1524 on the freedom of the will. Luther wrote, in answer, possibly his finest work, *The Bondage of the Will* (1525), in which he argued that the human will was enslaved to itself and its own interests, and needed deliverance by Christ to free it from itself in order freely to do good. The greatest disaster was the Peasants' War of 1525. The peasants in their grievous suffering identified the new cause of the Reformation with the amelioration of their social, civic and political grievances, legitimate in themselves. Though Luther had every sympathy with this cause, and a profound understanding, he would never permit the identification of the religious cause of the Reformation with the social cause of the peasants. The harm done to the true Reformation was immense and irreparable.

The next five years (1525–30) were marked by reconstruction and revitalization of the churches in Saxony. On the positive side Luther published his two catechisms in 1529, the Great Catechism and the Short Catechism.★ These years were marred by the controversy on the Lord's Supper between Zwingli and Luther. Luther held the Catholic view of the real presence (without transubstantiation), while Zwingli thought in terms

---

★ Readers of the present work would experience a powerful stimulus to their spirituality, as well as to their understanding of Christian doctrine and Christian ethics, from an examination of Luther's catechisms. Translations in *Luther's Primary Works*, ed. Wace and Buchheim (1896), pp. 1–156, and *Luther's Catechism*, trans. Robert H. Fischer (Philadelphia 1959).

LUTHER THE CHURCHMAN
(hearing the confession of his prince, and distributing
the Holy Communion, with Hus, to the royal family)
Credit: Mansell Collection

of a memorial feast. Luther would not yield, and the division is still with us. Protestantism had begun to exist as a separate entity when the evangelical princes 'protested' against the emperor at the Diet of Spires (1526), and gained authority to live and work as Protestants. In 1530 the Diet of Augsburg accepted the new Protestant 'Confession'. From then on we have Lutheranism.

Between 1532 and the death of Luther (1546) many attempts were made to reunite Christendom, notably at the Diet of Regensburg (1541), when agreement between Catholics and Protestants was arrived at even on the point of justification by faith only. Nevertheless, the document was a semantic compromise rather than theological agreement, and when the cardinals brought the document to Rome, it was abrogated by the pope.

Meanwhile, Luther continued to work, teach, preach and write in Wittenberg, and he died in 1546 while on a pastoral mission. His career had opened up in the pastoral concern for indulgences; it ended also in a pastoral ministry. History will always remember him as the father of the Reformation, scholar, writer, preacher, the man who defied pope and emperor and left a lasting impression on Europe, even the world. True all that is. Yet readers of the excerpts which follow may well discover that above all else he was a shepherd and pastor of souls.

This little book is no definitive study of Luther's theology, nor of his full religious faith. It speaks essentially of his spiritual breakthrough from late

LUTHER TOWARDS THE CLOSE OF HIS LIFE
(Note Cranach's representation standing full square
with Bible in hand)
Credit: Mary Evans Picture Library

medieval scholasticism within a secularized Church into the rediscovery of an evangelical biblical theology and all that meant for the reformation of the Church and the re-creation of a Christian ethic and a new society, above all, a Protestant spirituality.

The reader is advised first to read through the selections. These are set out in order of spiritual importance, beginning with the great central themes of faith, justification, law and gospel, word of God, and ending with the ethics and virtues which derive from these. This method gives a clearer idea of Luther. Subsequently, a page a day may be selected for consideration and meditation. The selections from Luther's writings and sayings have been chosen with one single purpose in mind: to help the general reader to deepen his spiritual life.

The writer makes bold to offer one suggestion. When the reader reflects on the transition of Luther from scholasticism to evangelical theology it might be worth considering it as a paradigm for the movement of the natural man in all of us to the new life in God intended by him in Christ for all of us: to take up our pilgrimage away from the aeon of Adam where we now live, into the aeon of Christ where we may begin to live; so to live in the kingdom of this world as to dwell in the Kingdom of God now, and, therefore, throughout eternity.

JAMES ATKINSON

Daily Readings with Martin Luther

The nature of faith

Abraham closed his eyes and hid himself in the darkness of faith, and therein he found light eternal.

In utter despair of everything, save Christ.

Faith is a free surrender and a joyous wager on the unseen, untried and unknown goodness of God.

If you believe, you already have God; if you do not believe, you do not have him. To have faith is to have God.

Faith unites the soul with the invisible, ineffable, unutterable, eternal, unthinkable word of God, while at the same time it separates it from all things visible and tangible.

Faith alone is able, under trial, to hear the deep, secret 'Yea' of God beneath and above his 'Nay'.

That most sweet stirring of the heart.

It is a living fountain springing up into life everlasting, as Christ describes it in John 4.

Faith – how it may be kindled

In seeking faith the soul gets grasped, yet does not itself grasp. That means, it is divested of its robes and shoes, indeed of all it possesses, even its dreams and fantasies, and is snatched by the Word . . . which immediately leads it into the desert.

To believe means to undertake to die.

Learn Christ and him crucified.

Faith means being zealous for God: in pious ignorance and intellectual darkness, without understanding, without feeling, without thinking, to wait upon God's activity.

Christ is the object of faith, nay rather, not the object, but if it may be said, the subject, the One present and active in the faith itself.

Though our faith may be weak, let us pray earnestly in company with the apostles, 'Lord, increase our faith', Luke 17:5, and with the father of the child in Mark 9:24, 'Lord, I believe: help thou my unbelief'.

The weakness of faith

There are two ways of believing. First, to believe *that* there is a God. This kind of faith is knowledge, or information, rather than faith as such. Secondly, there is faith *in* God. This faith I possess when I not only hold that what is said about God is true, but when I put my whole trust in him, undertake to deal with him personally, and believe without doubt that I shall find him to be and to do as I have been told.

Only faith of this kind, which, in the light of its knowledge about God, wagers its all on God, in life and in death, makes a man a true Christian and receives from God everything it desires.

To Melanchthon [a young professorial colleague of Luther, afraid of where it will all end]: You are worrying yourself sick because you cannot know how or where it will all end. But were you able to understand it all, then I would have nothing to do with this cause, much less be its leader.

God has put the matter in a word so homely that it does not exist in your vocabulary or learning, and that is faith. That is where all things that cannot be seen or grasped have been put (Hebrews 11:1).

If anybody does not like this, he can lump it. If Moses had insisted on understanding how he was to escape Pharaoh's army, Israel might still have been in Egypt today.

Justification – on being right with God

By the one solid rock we call the doctrine of justification by faith alone, we mean that we are redeemed from sin, death and the devil, and are made partakers of life eternal, not by self-help but by outside help, namely, by the work of the only-begotten Son of God, Jesus Christ alone.

God does not want to save us by our own personal and private righteousness and wisdom. He wants to save us by a righteousness and wisdom apart from this, other than this: a righteousness which does not come from ourselves, is not brought to birth by ourselves. It is a righteousness which comes into us from somewhere else.

It is not a righteousness which finds its origins in this world of ours.

As men without anything at all, we must wait for the pure mercy of God, we must wait for him to reckon us as righteous and wise.

As long as I recognize that I can in no way be righteous in the sight of God . . ., I then begin to ask for righteousness from him.

The only thing that resists this idea of justification is the pride of the human heart, proud through unbelief.

It does not believe because it does not regard the word of God as true. It does not regard it as true because it regards its own understanding as true, and the word of God runs contrary to that.

Justification – God's work, not ours

Unless a man is always humble, always distrustful of himself, unless he always fears his own judgement, his own feelings, his own will, he will to that extent be unable to stand for very long without falling.

Truth will pass him by.
Light and goodness will evade him.

We must conduct our lives as if we possessed nothing at all, and wait for the mercy of God to appear in all its stark nakedness. We must wait for *him* to reckon us as just and wise.

And this is precisely what God actually does, provided a man does not get there before God, by justifying himself and thinking that he is other than he really is.

I now possess another righteousness and life above this life, namely, Christ the Son of God, who knows no sin nor death, but is righteousness and life eternal.

Justification – in daily life

Paul is here (Romans 12) explaining spiritual progress and advancement. He is addressing people who are already Christians. Their life consists not in rest and quiet but in being on a journey from good to better. They are like a sick man advancing from sickness to health.

A man's existence is always in the state of moving from non-being, becoming, to being.

He is at one and the same time always in sin, in justification, in righteousness. Always a sinner, always penitent, always right with God.

The righteousness of God is not acquired by acts frequently repeated, as Aristotle taught, but is imparted by faith.

The good man knows that the good works he is doing are the outcome of faith of this kind, and are not his own works but God's works.

Christ is his wisdom, his righteousness, nay all that he is, has and does.

The justified man is most surely the work of Christ, the very tool of Christ.

The article concerning justification is master and prince of all doctrines. It rules over every man's conscience, and further, over the entire Church. Without it, the world is a dull place and full of darkness; without it, there is no error that does not creep in and take command.

Faith and works

There is something vital, energetic, active, mighty about this kind of faith! It is impossible for it not to be engaged in good works without ceasing. Nor does it first ask whether good works are to be done, but before one asks, faith has already spontaneously done them, and goes on doing them continuously.

Faith is a living, bold confidence in the grace of God, completely certain of itself.

In consequence, a man of faith becomes willing and anxious, without any prompting, to do good to all men, to serve the common good, to suffer all things for the love and praise of God, who has shown him such grace.

It will now be seen how it is impossible to separate works from faith, as impossible as it is to separate burning and shining from fire.

The Kingdom is within you. Decency, humility, truthfulness, chastity, in fact all the virtues, (and such truly constitute the Kingdom of God), cannot be imported by land or sea. They must blossom in the heart's soil.

Good works

Paul sets forth the whole life of a Christian man in Galatians 5:6, namely, that inwardly it consists of faith towards God, and outwardly in charity and good works to our neighbour.

In faith all works are equal, and any one work the same as any other.

God does not consider how little, or how great the works are, but God looks on the heart, which performs in faith and obedience to God the demands of its calling.

I cannot turn my neighbour away without turning God away: and that is to fall into unbelief.

We are, if I may be allowed so to express it, Christs to our neighbour.

God pays no heed to the insignificance of the work being done, but looks at the heart which is serving him in the work; and this is true of such mundane tasks as washing the dishes or milking the cows.

Christ – the work of God

The whole of Scripture deals with Christ, from beginning to end.

Every word of the Bible peals 'CHRIST'. Its whole concern is Christ.

Because Christ was born a man for our sake, and was sent by God to redeem us from sin and death, he must needs step into our place and become a sacrifice for us. He himself had to bear, and render satisfaction for, the wrath and the curse into which we had fallen and under which we lay.

You may ask, 'What then does it mean to know Christ?' Or, 'What benefits does he bring us?' The answer is that you begin to learn to know Christ when you begin to understand the words of St Paul in 1 Corinthians 1:30: thanks to God you have your existence in Christ Jesus. God is the source of your life in Christ Jesus, whom God made your wisdom, righteousness and sanctification and redemption.

It is Christ who has become for us the wisdom which is of God, as well as our justification, sanctification and redemption.

Christ – the way to God

Christ is of no benefit to you unless he be 'translated into words' for you.

Whatever is necessary for you to know is taught at best in Christ's humanity, for he is our Mediator, and no one can come to the Father except through him . . . and in him are all the treasures of wisdom and knowledge.[1]

One should think of no other God than Christ. The god who does not speak through Christ is no God at all.

Men seek God everywhere: but because they do not seek for him in Christ, they never find him.

No man can obtain Christ, the Bread of God, by dint of his own efforts. Neither will he find him by studying, hearing, asking, seeking. If we are truly to know Christ, all books are inadequate, all teachers incompetent, all intellects incapable. It is the Father himself who must reveal him, as Christ himself taught, 'No man can come to me, except the Father which hath sent me draw him: and I will raise him up at the Last Day.'[2]

[1] Colossians 2:3.
[2] John 6:44.

The soul must stay with Christ

My soul stays with Christ.

These are very precious, valuable and noteworthy words (John 6:32–35 on the Bread of Life), which we must not only know but turn them to our profit and say, 'With these words I shall go to bed in the evening and arise in the morning; on them I shall rely, on them I shall sleep, wake and work, and with them cross the final bridge of death into eternal life.'

Seek yourself only in Christ and not in yourself; then you will find yourself in him eternally.

The one doctrine which I have supremely at heart is that of faith in Christ, from whom, through whom and unto whom all my theological thinking flows back and forth, day and night.

To preach Christ means to feed the soul, to make it righteous, to set it free and to save it, if it believe the preaching. For faith alone is the saving and efficacious use of the word of God.[1]

Christ ought to be preached to the end that faith in him be established, that he may not only be Christ, but be Christ for you and for me, and that what is said of him, and what his name denotes, may be effectual in us.

[1] Romans 10:9; 10:4; 1:17; Habakkuk 2:4.

God

The condition of this life is not that of having God; rather, seeking him.

God hides his power in weakness, his wisdom in folly, his goodness in severity, his justice in sins, his mercy in anger.

God is saying to us:
him whom I am to help, I destroy;
him whom I want to quicken, save, enrich and make pious,
I mortify, reject, impoverish and reduce to nothing.[1]
But you refuse to accept such counsel and action from me.[2]

How then am I to help you?
What more can I do?[3]

Love is not of works, not human, no, nor even of angels, nor even of heaven, but is God himself.

Beyond all that this world affords, fear God, love him, and trust him to the end.

---

[1] Deuteronomy 32:30.
[2] Psalm 78:10–11.
[3] Isaiah 5:4.

God – hidden and revealed

The dispute with Erasmus was about the God who is hidden and the God who has revealed himself in Christ.

No faith in, no knowledge of, and no understanding of God, in so far as he is not revealed, are possible . . . the unrevealed God defies human investigation.

Nevertheless, the hidden God is none the less the revealed God, so that we may know him and apprehend him as our God.

Why God hides himself in the way he does we shall understand on that day when all enemies will have been put down under his feet.[1]

In the meantime all we have to do is to believe and to hope. For if one could see it now before one's eyes, there would be no need of faith.

It is the wisdom of the saints to believe in the truth in opposition to the lie, in the hidden truth against the manifest truth, in hope against hope.

[1] Corinthians 15:25.

The gospel – its cost

I have given up everything.

There is only one thing left, my weak and broken body.

If they take that away, they will make me the poorer by an hour of life, perhaps two hours.

Nevertheless, my soul they cannot take.

I know perfectly well that from the beginning of the world the word of Christ has been of such a kind that whoever wants to carry the gospel into the world must necessarily, like the apostles before them, renounce everything, even expect death at any and every hour.

If it were not so, it would not be the word of Christ.

By death the gospel was bought, by deaths spread abroad, by deaths safeguarded.

In like manner it must take many deaths to preserve it, even to restore it.

Christ is a bloody partnership for us.

The law and the gospel differentiated

In this verse (Psalm 85:5) the difference between Law and gospel is foreshadowed.

The Law is the word of Moses *to* us, the gospel is the word of God *within* us.

The former abides outside us: it addresses us in figures of speech, in forecasts of things to come.

The latter takes up its abode within us, and speaks of inward and spiritual things, and truth.

The one is speaking *within* us, the other speaks *to* us.

The righteousness of the Law is earthly, it is concerned with earthly affairs, and consists of our doing good works . . . The heavenly passive righteousness does not spring from our own efforts. We receive it from heaven. We do not produce it: we receive it in faith.

The Law is the ministry of the letter, the gospel the ministry of the Spirit: the letter killeth, but the Spirit giveth life.

The law and the gospel related

Why are we so feeble in faith that we more readily follow the feelings of sin and death maintained by the Law than turn to the laughter and joy of the gospel? . . .

The open jaws of hell terrify us more than the open gates of heaven elate us.

One thought of our sin causes us more sadness than almost all the sermons about the merits of Christ bring us joy.

In the trial of real anguish, the conscience should think of Christ, and know absolutely nothing but Christ only.

It should then exert its powers to the utmost to put the Law out of sight and mind, as far as it possibly can, and embrace nothing but Christ and his promises.

To say this is easy, I know. But to be able to do it in the hour of temptation, when the conscience is being handled by God, is the most difficult of all tasks.

The law fulfilled in the gospel

We establish the Law exactly as St Paul did, that is, we declare it fulfilled and confirmed by faith . . .

The Law is established in itself and in us. In itself, in so far as it is promulgated; in us, when we do it in will and in deed.

But, apart from faith, no one does this.

Therefore, we always make the covenant of God void and of non-effect, if we are without the grace given by faith in Christ.

In the Law many works are enjoined, and all external; but in the gospel there is only one, an internal work, and that is faith.

For that very reason the works of the Law make a righteousness which is external, but faith makes a righteousness hidden with God . . .

Nevertheless, both dispensations were given by God, but the old covenant was imposed until the day of fulfilment in the gospel.

Grace – *what it is*

I am seeking, searching, thirsting for nothing else than a gracious God.

Yet God continuously and earnestly offers himself as a God of grace,
and urges even those who spurn him and are his enemies, to accept him as such.

These promises of grace[1] are all based on Christ from the beginning of the world, so that God promises this grace to no one in any other way than in Christ and through Christ.

Christ is the messenger of God's promise to the entire world.

Grace consists in this:
that God is merciful to us,
shows himself gracious for the sake of the
Lord Christ, forgives all sins, and will not
impute them to us for eternal death.
That is grace: the forgiveness of sins for the
sake of the Lord Christ,
the covering-up of all sins.

Grace makes the Law dear to us.
And then, sin is no more there,
and the Law is no longer against us,
but with us.

[1] John 1:17.

Grace – how it works

All the many countless blessings which God gives us here on earth are merely those gifts which last for a time.

But his grace and loving regard are the inheritance which endures throughout eternity . . .

In giving us such gifts here on earth he is giving us only those things that are his own, but in his grace and love towards us he gives his very self.

In receiving his gifts we touch but his hand; but in his gracious regard we receive his heart, his spirit, his mind, his will.

Man receives grace immediately and fully. In this way he is saved. Good works are not necessary to assist him in this: they follow. It is as if God were to produce a fresh, green tree out of a dry log, which tree would then bear its natural fruit.

The Bible – how to understand it

It is most certain that the Holy Scriptures cannot be fathomed by study and scholarship alone.

Therefore, your first duty in approaching the Bible is to begin to pray, and to pray to this effect:

That if it pleases God to accomplish something through you for his own glory, and not for your own glory nor that of any other man, that of his grace he grant you a true understanding of his words.

The reason for this is that no master of the divine word exists, except the author of these words, as Christ himself says, 'They shall all be taught of God.'[1]

Therefore, you on your part must stand in complete despair of your own industry and scholarship, and rely solely and utterly on the inspiration of the Holy Spirit.

Believe me, I know the truth of this in my own life.

[1] John 6:45.

The Bible as the word of God

Let the man who wants to hear *God* speak read Holy Scripture.

Whenever a man reads the word of God, he is being handled by God: the Holy Spirit is speaking to him.

Every word of God terrifies us, yet at the same time it comforts us; it hurts, yet it heals; it breaks down, yet it builds up; it plucks up, yet it plants; it humbles, yet it exalts.[1]

The word of God created heaven and earth and all things visible and invisible. It is that same word which must effect reformation, not we poor sinners.

Is it not true to say that God's word is greater and more important than faith? For God's word is not founded and built on faith, but on the contrary, faith is built on God's word. Besides, our faith may waver, even fail altogether, but the word of God stands for ever.

I have always with the greatest diligence exhorted men to read Scripture and to hear the spoken word, that we may deal with the God who has revealed himself and is speaking to us, and may in every way avoid the God who is silent and hidden in majesty.

---

[1] Jeremiah 1:10.

The daily life – a pilgrimage to heaven

This life is not a state of being righteous, but rather, of growth in righteousness;

not a state of being healthy,
but a period of healing;

not a state of being,
but becoming;

not a state of rest,
but of exercise and activity.

We are not yet what we shall be,
but we grow towards it;

the process is not yet finished,
but is still going on;

this life is not the end,
it is the way to a better.

All does not yet shine with glory;
nevertheless, all is being purified.[1]

[1]   2 Corinthians 3:18.

Prayer – as human activity

Listen quietly, and do not present any impediment of your own thoughts, for the Holy Ghost himself is preaching when you are at prayer, and one word of his preaching is better than a thousand words of our praying.

We should pray, not as the custom is, turning over many pages or counting many beads, but fixing our mind upon some pressing need; desire it with all earnestness, and exercise faith and confidence towards God in the matter, in such a way that we do not doubt but that we shall be heard.

Prayer is, therefore, a special exercise of faith, and faith makes the prayer so acceptable that either it will be surely granted, or something better than we ask will be given in its stead.[1]

A Christian is always praying, whether he is sleeping or waking, for his heart is always praying, and even a little sigh is a great and mighty prayer.

[1] James 1:6f; Mark 11:24; Luke 11:9ff.

Prayer as God's activity

Prayer is a two-way activity. First, we speak to God, and then he speaks to us. Simply talk with God – that is the nature of prayer. How great and glorious a thing it is that the most high God in all his majesty so condescends to us poor worms of earth that we may open our mouths to talk to him, and that he delights to listen. Yet more glorious and precious by far it is that he does actually speak to us, and that we listen to him.

Scripture calls both activities respectively the spirit of grace and the spirit of prayer. Remember that God is the author of both – he not only permits us to speak to him through prayer, but he actually converses with us through the spirit of grace. A Christian must be as certain that God hears his prayer as he is certain that he truly cleaves to him and believes in him . . . and be as far removed from doubt concerning prayer as he is in God's word, be he a preacher or a hearer of the same.

Always make a good and hearty 'Amen', and never doubt that God hears you and says 'Yes!' to your prayer. Further, always bear in mind that you are not standing or kneeling alone but the whole of Christendom is standing or kneeling with you. It is the word of God and his promise which makes good your prayer, not your own devotion.

Luther at prayer

Almighty and everlasting God, what a world is this we live in! . . . How small and trivial is man's trust in God! How frail and weak the flesh! How strong and active the devil through his apostles and minions with all their worldly wisdom! How soon the world abandons us and goes its way, the way of all flesh, the broad road that leads to hell, where the ungodly belong. Yes, how it esteems nothing but pomp and circumstance, might and power! If I do but turn an eye in that direction, it is all over with me and my doom is pronounced upon me. O God, my own God, be my succour against all the reason and wisdom of the world! You alone must do it, you alone. For, after all, it is not my cause but yours. I put not my confidence in any man . . . Was it for this you chose me? I ask the question, yet I know for certain that you have chosen me . . . God's will be done! . . .

The cause is just, and it is your cause. For this reason I am resolved never to part from you till the end of time. This is my decision, in your name I make it. If ruin and destruction do befall my body in this cause (yet my body is your creation and your handiwork), your word and your Spirit are sufficient for me . . . So help me God, Amen.

Luther's prayer on his deathbed
(1546)

O heavenly Father, God of all comfort, I thank thee that thou hast revealed to me thy beloved Son, Jesus Christ, in whom I have believed, whom I have preached and confessed, whom I have loved and praised . . .

I pray thee, dear Lord Christ, let me commend my soul to thee.

O heavenly Father, if I leave this body and depart this life, I am certain that I will be with thee for ever and ever, and that I can never, never tear myself out of thy hands.

So God loved the world that he gave his only-begotten Son, Jesus Christ, that whosoever believeth in him should not perish, but have eternal life.[1] [This text Luther repeated three times.]

Father, into thy hands I commend my spirit. Thou hast redeemed me, thou true God. Amen.

[1] John 3:16.

The Church

In the communion of saints we are all brothers and sisters so closely united that a closer relationship cannot be conceived. For in this fellowship we have one baptism, one Christ, one sacrament, one food, one gospel, one faith, one Spirit, one spiritual body; and each is a member one of another. No other society is so deeply rooted, so closely knit. For, while natural brothers possess one flesh, one heritage, one home, nevertheless, eventually they must part from one another and merge with another heritage and another blood in marriage.

We are all one with the holy fathers and prophets of the Old Testament; they looked for the promise and believed in it; we see it and believe in it.

The people of God, in other words, the Church, are simply those who rely on nothing else but God's grace and mercy.

The spiritual tyrants have turned Christendom into a temporal power.

God cannot, and God will not allow anybody but himself to rule the soul of man.

The hidden Church

You cannot say of the Church, 'Lo! here it is!', or 'There!' Christ clearly says, The Kingdom of God is within you, and, The Kingdom of God cometh not with observation,[1] and, That which is born of the Spirit is Spirit.[2] Christ clearly says that there is no locality, place or any external mark of the Kingdom of God; it is not here or there, but is a spirit within us.

[Luther no 'Lutheran'.] What is Luther? My doctrine is not my own invention, of that I am certain. Nor have I been crucified for anyone . . . How can I, poor, foul carcass that I am, come to have men give to the children of Christ a name derived from my worthless name? No! No! No!, my dear friends. Let us call ourselves Christians, after him whose doctrine we hold.

Although Christians do have some distinguishing external marks, given them by Christ, namely, baptism, the sacrament of the altar and the preaching of the gospel, even these marks may deceive us in judging particular individuals. For many a man has been baptized, hears the gospel, and goes to communion with all the others, but is none the less a scoundrel and no Christian. A man's spirituality can only be recognized by that faith within the heart which considers Christ its Good Shepherd and hears his voice.

[1] Luke 17:20f; John 3:6; also Romans 2:11.
[2] John 1:13.

The Church upheld by word and sacrament

The Christian communion has this promise: that the Holy Ghost will abide with them forever.[1] But there is still more. He will also teach believers, and call Christ's words to their remembrance continuously till the Last Day. This we confess in the Creed: I believe in the Holy Ghost, and in the holy Catholic Church, and all therein. With these words we affirm that the Holy Ghost dwells in Christendom and sanctifies it, and does so by word and sacrament, by which means he creates faith within us, as well as knowledge of Christ. The word and sacrament are his tools, so to speak, the means by which *he* continuously sanctifies and purifies Christendom, without rest or respite. This is the way *he* makes Christians holy and acceptable in the sight of God, not at all by virtue of what we do for ourselves, nor even by virtue of what we are, but simply because the Holy Ghost has been given us.

The Church is maintained only by its preachers, and they are made by God . . . it would have perished long ago had it depended on its bishops.

Where Christ is not preached, there is no Holy Spirit to form the Christian Church.

Let him who wants a true and pure Church cling to the word, by which everything is upheld.

[1] John 14:16.

The priesthood of all believers

It is pure human invention to argue that pope, bishops, priests and monks are to be called the 'spiritual estate'; princes, lords and artisans the 'temporal estate' . . . All Christians are of the 'spiritual estate', and there is no difference between them at all, except one of office. Paul says, We are all one body, yet every member has its own work, whereby it serves every other member, all because we have one baptism, one gospel, one faith, and are all alike Christians:[1] for baptism, gospel and faith alone make us 'spiritual' and a Christian people.

Although we are all priests, this does not mean that all of us may preach, teach and rule. Certain ones from the community must be selected and set apart for such office. He who holds such office is not a priest by virtue of his office but is servant to all the others, who are as equally priests as he is . . .

The Scriptures make us all priests alike, but the church priesthood now universally distinguished from 'the laity', and alone called a priesthood, is described in the Scriptures as a ministry, a service, an office, an eldership, a fostering, a guardianship, a preaching office, a shepherd or pastor.

Through baptism we are all consecrated priests.[2]

[1] Corinthians 12:12ff.
[2] 1 Peter 2:9.

The two kingdoms

Christ did not come to establish any temporal kingdom, for the promises of God are altogether far too glorious for that sort of thing. It would not well befit our Lord to establish such a kingdom. Christ is not concerned with political and domestic economy, but is a King who came to destroy the dominion of the devil, and to save mankind. Our prayers should be: Give temporal kingdom and crown to whom you will, grant only this to me, that I shall not die eternally. I shall be satisfied with but little, if only I am secure against death and eternal damnation . . . But only Christ can effect this, and this is the real treasure and heritage Christ brings to all men.

I must always drive in and hammer home the distinction between these two kingdoms . . . for the cursed devil himself does not cease to cook and brew these two kingdoms into one dish. In the devil's kingdom the secular lord is always wanting to teach and instruct Christ how he should run his Church and the spiritual government. By the same token, the false and factious agitators, though not in God's name, always want to teach and instruct the secular rulers how they are to govern . . . All this is just to confuse and mingle into one secular and spiritual government.

The minister of state is 'God's left hand'. His work is not simply a matter of human order or appointment. His is a divinely ordered office.

The world

The world and the masses are and always will be unChristian, even though they be baptized and Christian in name. Hence, a man who would venture to govern an entire community or the world with the gospel would be like a shepherd who wants to put wolves, lions, eagles and sheep all in one fold. The sheep would keep the peace all right, but they would not last long. The world cannot be ruled with a rosary.

O God! O God! O my God! You who are my God, support me in this struggle against the reason and wisdom of all the world. You do it! You must do it, and you only. This affair is not mine but thine.

The world is always true to itself; by nature it is unbelieving, the kingdom of Satan, the enemy of Christ.

We are guests at an inn whose keeper is a villain.

In God's purpose this world is only a preparation and scaffolding for the life of the world to come.

Why do we tremble before the world as before a triumphant conqueror? It is worth going to Rome or Jerusalem on one's knees to hear those words of Christ, 'Be of good cheer; I have overcome the world.'[1]

[1] John 16:33.

The sacraments – prefigured in the Bible

It is a mistake to think that the sacraments of the New Testament differ from those of the Old with respect to the efficacy of what they signify.

What both signify is equally efficacious, for the same God who now saves us through baptism and the Lord's Supper saved Abel through his sacrifice, Noah by means of the rainbow, Abraham through circumcision, and all the others through his appointed signs . . .

Both our signs of the sacraments and the signs given to the patriarchs have each a word of promise attached to them. This word calls for faith; it cannot be fulfilled by any other work we might devise.

Therefore, these are signs or sacraments of justification, sacraments of justifying faith and not of any work to be performed.

It follows that their entire efficacy consists in faith itself, not in the doing of a work.

Whoever believes them fulfils them, even though he perform no work at all.

Neither sacrament nor priest but faith in the word of Christ, mediated through the priest in his office, justifies you.

The sacraments – what they are

It is appropriate that those rites be called sacraments which contain promises with signs attached to them. The others, which have no appointed sign attached, remain simply promises. It follows, therefore, strictly speaking, that there are only two sacraments in the Church of God: baptism and the bread, for it is in these two only that we note both the divinely instituted sign and the promise of forgiveness of sins. The sacrament of penance, which I myself once counted among these two, lacks the visible and divinely instituted sign, and as I have argued, amounts to no more than a return to baptism.

The best and greatest part of the sacraments is the word and covenant of God. Without these the sacraments are dead and worthless, as a body without a soul, a cask without wine, a purse without money, a promise without fulfilment, a letter without spirit, a sheath without a knife . . .

If you leave out the word, baptism is nothing but water, and the Lord's Supper simply bread; for the word is the kernel of the sacrament.

The sacraments are not fulfilled by being done, but by being believed.

The sacraments in daily life

Imagine how many people there are who would like to be certain of the Christian faith, or would like a sign from heaven telling them how they stand with God, and whether they are of the elect. But what help would it be to them if they still would not believe? What good are all the signs without faith? What help are the venerable signs of the sacraments in today's world, or even the very words of God for that matter, if received with unbelief? Why do people not hold to the common sacraments, the sure and appointed signs? They have been tested and tried by all the saints before us, found reliable by all who believed, who in their faith in them received all that they promised.

In the sacraments we see nothing marvellous – just water, bread and wine, the words of a mere preacher. There is nothing special about that. But learn to believe what a glorious majesty lies hidden under these despised things. It is exactly the same with the Lord Christ in his incarnation. We see a frail, weak mortal, yet he is the very majesty of God himself. In just the same way God himself speaks to us and deals with us in these most common and despised elements.

Baptism

It is not the water which works the blessings of forgiveness of sins, delivering from death and the devil and giving eternal salvation, but the word of God which is in and with the water. Without the word of God the water is simply water, no baptism takes place. But with the word of God it is a true baptism: it is the water of life graciously outpoured, a washing of regeneration in the Holy Ghost.[1]

Take away the word of God, the water is no different from what the maidservant uses in the kitchen. When it is there as God ordained, then it is a sacrament and is called 'Christ's baptism'. Water and word do not work our salvation magically. Taken together they are a treasure which he grants us, a treasure which faith receives.

Throughout the course of life every Christian has enough to learn and practise about baptism, for he has always to see that he steadfastly believes what it promises and carries with it: victory over death and the devil, remission of sin, the grace of God, Christ in all his fullness, and the Holy Ghost with all his gifts.

My first words when the devil assaults me – 'I have been baptized!'

[1] Titus 3:4–8.

The Eucharist

The bread, the word, the spiritual meat are none other than Christ himself. As our Lord himself declares in John 6, 'I am the living bread which came down from heaven to give life to the world . . .'

No one can procure this bread by dint of his own efforts, not even by hearing, studying, asking, searching. If we are truly to learn to know Jesus Christ, then all books fall short, all teachers are too feeble, all reason too limited. The Father himself must reveal him and present him to us, as Christ further says in John 6, 'No one can come to me unless the Father who sent me draws him . . .'[1] In the sacrament Christ is received.

True as this is, it would not happen if Christ were not, at the same time, prepared and proclaimed by the word. The word brings Christ to the people, and acquaints their hearts with him . . . Therefore, we should preach Christ only, and relate everything to him . . . Christ was given us by God to be our wisdom, righteousness, sanctification and redemption.[2]

When Christ is proclaimed, and the precious bread distributed in this way, the souls of men will lay hold of it . . . However, he will be of no benefit to you, nor will you be able to avail yourself of him, unless God himself translates him into words whereby you can hear and know him.

[1] John 6:44, 45, 65.
[2] 1 Corinthians 1:30.

The Eucharist explained

Think of the sacrament in the same way you think of the person of Christ. In order that the Godhead dwell in him, it is not necessary for the human nature to be transubstantiated and the Godhead contained within the human accidents, but since both natures are present in their entirety, it is true to say, 'This man is God', and 'This God is man'. Though philosophy does not grasp this, faith does; and the authority of God's word is greater than the grasp of the human intellect.

So is it with the sacrament. In order that the real Body and the real Blood may be in the sacrament, it is not necessary that the bread and wine be transubstantiated, and Christ contained under their accidents. Both remain there together, and it is truly said, 'This bread is my Body; this wine is my Blood'.

Grace is a given thing, given equally in word and in sacrament. God's word is a sacrament, no less than the sacrament his word. I would sooner drink blood with the pope than mere wine with Zwingli.

When you come to communion, fully confess that you have nothing to give to God, but that all things come from him, in particular, eternal life and righteousness in him.

The Eucharist experienced

When the priest administers this sacrament to us
he ministers Christ to us, and in Christ we are
incorporated into the fellowship of all saints. In
partaking of this sacrament, all self-seeking love
is rooted out. It gives place to that love which
seeks the common good. In our mutual love we
find one bread, one drink, one body, one
community, and in that love lies the true union
of Christian brethren. The sacrament has no
blessing and no significance unless love grows
daily and so changes a man that he is made one
with all others . . . In the sacrament we become
united with Christ, and are made one body with
all the saints.

The mere recitation of the Creed in the
communion service is as good as hearing a
sermon, for it teaches people to believe in Christ.
In the very act of confessing the Creed a
communicant is working for the increase and pres-
ervation of the Church of Christ, the furtherance
of the gospel and the sacrament, the conversion
of sinners, the destruction of the power of Satan.
Steadfastly to love God and one's neighbour is as
great a thing as raising the dead.

For us the sacrament is a ford, a bridge, a door,
a ship, a litter, in which and by means of which
we pass from this world into eternal life. Therefore, all depends on faith.

The Eucharist in daily life

God appointed this twofold form of bread and wine, rather than any other, as a further indication of the union and fellowship which takes place in the sacrament. There is no union more intimate, deep and inseparable than the union of food with him who partakes of it, since food enters the system, is changed into his nature and becomes one with his being. Other unions, such as those effected by nails, glue, ropes and the like, do not make one indivisible substance of the objects joined together. In like manner we are united with Christ in the sacrament, and at the same time incorporated into the fellowship of the communion of saints.

The Lord's Supper deals with individuals. In the administration the Body of Christ is given to you in particular under the form of bread and wine, while you as an individual person are told that his Body was given for *you* and that his Blood was shed for *you*. This is said so that, nothing doubting, you may appropriate this sacrifice as your very own, because it is placed into your mouth and made your own, to eat and drink for yourself only. In this act of communing, God is certainly dealing with and speaking not just to all persons in general, but to you as an individual in particular.

The cross

The cross teaches us to believe in hope even when there is no hope. The wisdom of the cross is deeply hidden in a profound mystery. In fact, there is no other way to heaven than taking up the cross of Christ. On account of this we must beware that the active life with its good works, and the contemplative life with its speculations, do not lead us astray. Both are most attractive and yield peace of mind, but for that very reason they hide real dangers, unless they are tempered by the cross and disturbed by adversaries. The cross is the surest path of all. Blessed is the man who understands this truth.

It is a matter of necessity that we be destroyed and rendered formless, so that Christ may be formed within us, and Christ alone be in us . . . Real mortifications do not happen in lonely places away from the society of other human beings. No! They happen in the home, the market place, in secular life . . . 'Being conformed to Christ' is not within our powers to achieve. It is God's gift, not our own work.

He who is not *crucianus*, if I may coin a word, is not *Christianus*: in other words, he who does not bear his cross is no Christian, for he is not like his Master, Jesus Christ.

The cross – true peace of mind

You do indeed 'seek peace and ensure it', but altogether in the wrong way. You seek the peace the world gives, not the peace Christ gives.

Are you not aware, my dear father prior, how God is so wonderful among his people that he has set his peace where there is no peace, that is in the midst of all our trials? As he says, 'Rule thou in the midst of thine enemies'.

It is not, therefore, that man whom no one bothers who has peace. That kind of peace is the peace the world gives. It is that man whom everyone disturbs and everyone harasses, and yet, who joyfully and quietly endures them all.

You are saying with Israel, 'Peace! Peace!' when there is no peace. Say, rather, with Christ, 'Cross! Cross!' and there is no cross. For the cross ceases to be a cross the moment you say gladly, 'Blessed cross! Of all the trees that are in the wood there is none such as thee!'

Seek this peace and you will find peace. Seek for nothing else than to take on trials with joy. Seek them as you would holy relics. You will never find this peace by seeking and choosing what you feel and judge to be the path of peace.

The cross – a way of life

Therefore, my dear friar, learn Christ and him crucified. Learn to despair of your own efforts and learn to pray to him, learn to cry to him: 'Lord Jesus, thou art my righteousness, but I am thy sin. Thou hast taken upon thyself what is mine, and hast given me what is thine: thou hast taken upon thyself what thou wast not, and hast given me what I was not.'

Beware of aspiring to a righteousness of such purity that you would not wish to be looked upon as a sinner, or, still worse, not to be one! For Christ dwells only in sinners. It was for this very reason he descended from heaven, where he had his dwelling with the righteous, to dwell among us poor sinners on earth. Meditate on love of such power, and you will then experience his consolation of love.

Why did he have to die if we can of ourselves find a good conscience by means of our own works and self-imposed afflictions?

You will never find peace of mind except in Christ alone, and even then, only when you have despaired of yourself and of your own works.

You will also learn from him that just in the manner he has accepted you, so has he made your sins his own, and also his righteousness your own.

The cross – in practice

The apostle teaches, Receive one another, as Christ also received us to the glory of God.[1] And again, Let this mind be in you which was also in Christ Jesus: who, though he was in the form of God, did not count equality with God a thing to be grasped, but emptied himself, taking the form of a servant . . . obedient unto . . . death on a cross.[2] In like manner, if you think of yourself as on a higher level of spirituality than they, do not reckon this righteousness as booty to be snatched at, as if it were your own, but humble yourself, forget what you are, and, after the fashion of Christ, be as one of them so that you can help them.

Pray for whatever you lack, kneeling before Christ. Christ will teach you all things. This one thing do: keep your eyes fixed on that which he has done for you and for all men so that you may learn what you should do for others. If Christ had sought to live only among nice people, and to die only for his friends, with whom would he have ever lived, for whom then would he have died? Go and do thou likewise, my dear friar, and continue to pray for me. The Lord be with you. Farewell in the Lord.

[1] Romans 15:7.
[2] Philippians 2:5ff.

The theology of the cross

A true theologian understands the phrase 'the visible and hinder parts of God'[1] to mean the passion and the cross . . . The 'invisible parts' mean the humanity of God, his weakness, his foolishness. It is Paul's description, 'the weakness and foolishness of God'.[2] Because men put to wrong use the knowledge of God which they had gleaned from his work of creation, God determined to be known from sufferings. He sought to condemn that kind of knowledge of the things invisible which was based on a wisdom derived from things visible; so that, in this way, those who did not worship God as made known in his works, might worship him hidden behind his sufferings. 'For, seeing that in the wisdom of God the world did not know God by means of its wisdom, it was God's good pleasure to save those who believe by the foolishness of the preaching.'[3] From now on, it could never be enough for a man, nor could it benefit him, to know God in his glory and majesty unless at the same time he knows him in the humility and shame of the cross. 'Verily thou art a hidden God.'[4]

'Philip, whoever sees me sees my Father.'[5] In Christ crucified is the true theology and the true knowledge of God.

[1] Deuteronomy 33:23.
[2] 1 Corinthians 1:25.
[3] 1 Corinthians 1:21, 27–29.
[4] Isaiah 45:15.
[5] John 14:9.

Unbelief or half-belief

In the very act of affirming my faith, my God and Father suffers me to be thrown into prison, drowned, beheaded. It is then my faith falters, and in a moment of weakness I cry, 'Who knows whether it is really true?' . . .

At such a moment we must say, 'Let go of everything in which I have trusted'. And then turn to God and say, 'Lord, you alone give help and comfort. You have said that you would help me. I believe your word. O my God and Lord, I have heard from you a joyful and comforting word. I hold to that word. I know you cannot lie to me. No matter how you may appear to me, you will keep the word you have promised. That, and nothing else.'

The story of the Canaanite woman[1] shows us how deeply God can hide his face from us, and how we should not judge God according to our subjective feeling and thinking about him, but *only* in accordance with his word. All Christ's answers sounded like 'No!', yet he pronounced no final 'No!' He had not said that she was *not* of the House of Israel. He had not said that she was a *dog*. He never actually said 'No!' Yet, all his answers sounded more like 'No!' than 'Yes!' Our hearts feel the same in the hour of trial. We see nothing but a plain 'No!' Therefore, underneath and beyond the 'No!', grasp the deeply hidden 'Yes!' Hold on, as the woman did, to God's word.

[1] Matthew 15:27–28.

Doubt and uncertainty

God is invisible, inscrutable, incomprehensible, and so on . . . Give up all such speculating, which is utterly unrelated to the word of God anyhow. God is saying to you, From the unrevealed God I shall become your own revealed God: I shall incarnate my own beloved Son . . . 'This is my beloved Son. Hear you him.'[1] Behold his death, his cross, his passion. See him hanging on his mother's breast, and hanging on the cross. What Christ says and does, you may be sure of. 'No man cometh to the Father but by me.'[2] 'He that hath seen me hath seen the Father.'[3] What God is saying to you is this: 'Here in Christ you have me, here in Christ you will see me.'

If you want to escape from despair and hatred of God, let speculation go. Begin with God *from the bottom upwards, not from the top downwards*. In other words, begin with Christ incarnate, and with your own terrible original sin. There is no other way. Otherwise, you will remain a doubter for the rest of your life.

At all costs cling to the revealed God. Allow no one to take the child Jesus from you. Hold fast to Christ, and you will *never* be lost. God the Father longs for you. God the Son wishes to be your Saviour, your Liberator. In this kind and lovely manner has God freed us from these terrible assaults and trials.

[1]   Matthew 17:5.
[2]   John 14:6.
[3]   John 14:9.

Suffering

No misfortune we experience in this life can do any injury to our soul. Quite the contrary! Misfortune serves to our advantage. St Paul says, 'We know that all things work together for good to them that love God, to them who are called according to his purpose.'[1] In our bodies we suffer woe, and it must always be so, for we would not be true Christians if we did not suffer with Christ, and if we were without sympathy for those who suffer.

Those who inflict the greatest harm on believers are their greatest benefactors, as long as they bear their sufferings in the right spirit.

If we are to suffer, then let it be suffering which God inflicts upon us, and not that which we choose to impose upon ourselves, for he knows best what suffering will help and serve us.

Wherever Christ is, Judas, Pilate, Herod, Caiaphas and Annas will inevitably be there also, and the cross for good measure.

You are still assailed by terror and unbelief. Accept this scourge as laid upon you by God for your own good, as Paul had to endure a thorn in the flesh,[2] and thank God that he deems you worthy of this feeling, for this will drive you all the more to prayer, and to seek help from God.

---

[1] Romans 8:28.
[2] Read 2 Corinthians 12:7–10.

The troubled heart

If you are living without faith and with a guilty conscience, you will encounter in all the experiences of life the very God from whom you are fleeing.

My conscience is captive to the word of God.

As to the truth of my opinions, I would most readily recant, both at your command and on the advice of my vicar-general, if my conscience in any way allowed it. But I know in my heart that neither your command nor his advice, nor the influence of anyone else, ought to force me to act against my conscience. In fact, no person and no event could make me so act.

If you find yourself unable to believe this, entreat God for faith. Spur yourself on to believe! Stop contemplating the suffering of Christ (for clearly this has already done its work and filled you with fear), but pass beyond that and contemplate his friendly heart, and how this heart beats with such love towards you that it impels him to bear with pain your conscience and your sin. Your heart will swell with love for him, and the confidence of faith will be strengthened. Go further! Rise beyond the heart of Christ to the heart of God, and you will then see that Christ would not have shown such love towards you had God not, in his eternal love, wanted this, for the love Christ shows to you stems from his obedience to God.

Sin

In the sins instanced in the Ten Commandments we see nothing else but self-love, which seeks its own interests, takes from God what is his, from men what is theirs, and from all it is, has and does, gives nothing back to God or man. St Augustine well says, 'The beginning of all sin is the love of one's own self . . .' Therefore, he lives best who in no wise lives for himself, and he who lives for himself, lives worst.

Be a sinner, and sin boldly; but more boldly still, believe in Christ and rejoice in him, for he is victorious over sin, death and the world. As long as we live in this world we are bound to sin . . . but no sin will separate us from Christ. Pray boldly – for you, too, are a mighty sinner.[1]

If you have the presumption to try to quiet your conscience with your own contrition and penitence, you will never come to peace of mind, but will, rather, end up in despair. If we allow sin to remain in our conscience and try to deal with it there, or if we look at sin in our heart, it will prove much too strong for us, and will remain for ever. But, if we look at it as borne by Christ, and see it overcome in his resurrection, and have the courage to believe this, it is in that very act dead, brought to naught. Sin cannot remain in Christ, for it is swallowed up in his resurrection.

[1] Luther is, of course, not exhorting to sin but to faith and action in faith, even if, as a sinner, his good deeds are tainted with sin.

Bereavement

I have been urged by friends of yours to write to you. Please receive this letter kindly. They tell me that since the death of your dear wife, who departed this life at peace with God, you have been trying to help the repose of her soul with good works and services, particularly with masses for the dead and vigils . . .

First, I beg to remind you of what Job says: 'The Lord gave, and the Lord has taken away; as it seemed good to the Lord, so has he done.'[1] You should sing the same song to God, a loving and faithful God who gave you a loving and faithful wife, and has now taken her away. She was his before he gave her; she was his after he had given her; and she still remains his (as we all do), even now that he has taken her away.

Although it hurts us when he takes his own from us, his good will should be a greater comfort to us than all his gifts, for God is immeasurably more than all his gifts. Although we cannot perceive God's will as clearly as we can see a wife, yet we can perceive and apprehend his will by faith.

Cheerfully give back to God what is his, and accept this proper exchange, this strange barter whereby, instead of a dear, kindly wife, you have in exchange a dear, kindly will of God. Nay, more! God himself. Truly, God's goodness and mercy extend beyond this life.

---

[1] Job 1:21.

Death

At birth a child comes forth amid pain and danger, from the narrow dwelling of the mother's womb, into the broad light of day. In a similar way a man goes through the narrow gate of death when he departs this life. And though heaven and earth under which we now live appear so wide, so vast, yet, in comparison with the heaven that shall be, it is far narrower and much smaller than is the womb in comparison with the broad expanse of heaven. That is why the death of saints is called a new birth, and their festivals birthdays. A woman, when she is in travail, has sorrow, because her hour is come; but as soon as she is delivered of the child, she remembers no more the anguish for joy that a man is born into the world. Likewise in death. We wrestle in anguish, yet know that hereafter we shall come forth into a wide, open space, and into eternal joy.

When I feel the dread of death, I say, 'O death, you have nothing to do with me, because I have another death which kills my death. And the death which kills is stronger than that which is killed.'

God appointed death to be the destroyer of death. It is evidence for God's surpassing goodness, that after death has entered,[1] it is not permitted to hurt us *ultimately*, but is taken captive at the outset, and made to be the punishment and death of sin.

[1] Genesis 3:19.

A Christmas sermon[1]

Note how simply these events happen on earth, yet so highly regarded in heaven! There is the poor, young wife Mary, living in Nazareth, thought nothing of and regarded as one of the lowliest women in the town. No one is aware of the mighty wonder she is carrying. She herself keeps silent and says nothing, makes nothing of it, and thinks of herself as the lowliest woman in town. She sets off with Joseph her master . . . As they draw nigh to Bethlehem the evangelist presents them to us as the most wretched and disregarded of all the pilgrims, being forced to give way to everyone, till at last they are shown into a stable, and made to share shelter, table and bedroom with the beasts. While all this is going on, many a wicked man sits in the inn above and is treated like a lord. Not a soul notices, not a soul understands what God is doing in the stable. He leaves empty the palaces and stately homes, he leaves the masses to their eating and drinking and good cheer. Consequently, the comfort and treasure in Christ remain hidden from the likes of such people. O! what a thick, black darkness hung over Bethlehem that night, when she failed to apprehend so great a light within her walls! How decisively God shows that he has no regard for the world and its ways, what it is, what it has and what it does! How truly the world shows for its part that it has no regard for God, what he is, what he has, what he does . . .

[1] Luke 2:1–14.

A Christmas thought[1]

To the Kingdom of Christ belong only poor, suffering men. It was for their sake that this King came down from heaven to earth. Therefore is his Kingdom a kingdom for hearts which are fearful, sorrowful and miserable. To such I now preach, just as the angel preached to the poor, frightened shepherds: 'Behold, I bring you good tidings of great joy!'

True enough, this great joy is offered to all people, yet it can be received only by those who have a troubled conscience and a grieving heart. The angel is saying, 'To those I have come, for such people is my message, to them my good tidings.'

Is it not a great miracle, that where the anxiety of conscience is greatest shall this joy be nearest; that where you are disheartened by fear and anxiety there shall come such sweet and abundant joy, that the human heart is too narrow to comprehend it? . . .

Listen to the angel's song, all you who have a troubled heart. 'I bring you good tidings of great joy!' Never let the thought cross your mind that Christ is angry with you! He did not come to condemn you. If you want to define Christ rightly, then pay heed to how the angel defines him, namely, 'A great joy!'

[1] Luke 2:1–14.

An Easter sermon

O death, where is thy sting? O grave, where is
thy victory? This is so true that even Satan cannot
deny it. Christ's resurrection and victory over sin,
death and hell is greater than all heaven and earth.
You can never imagine his resurrection and
victory so great but that in actuality it is far, far
greater. For as his person is mighty, eternal,
without limit, incomprehensible, so also is his
resurrection, victory and triumph mighty, eternal,
without limit, incomprehensible. Were hell a
thousand times more, and death ten thousand
times more, it would all but a spark, a mere
drop, compared with Christ's resurrection, victory and triumph. But, his resurrection, victory
and triumph gives Christ to all who believe in
him. Since we have been baptized in his name,
and believe in him, it follows that even if you
and I underwent sin, death and hell a hundred
thousandfold, it would amount to nothing; for
Christ's resurrection, victory and triumph, which
have been given me in the baptism and in the
word by faith, and therefore are my own, are
infinitely greater. If this is true, and I most
certainly believe it to be true, then let sin, death
and hell dog my steps and growl at me. What will
they do to us? What can they do? What?

A Whitsunday sermon

Christ is hastening to his conclusion, that he is about to rise to his feet and go forth to his passion.[1] All that he had hitherto said had been spoken at table. He is saying, 'I have said many good things to you, to comfort and strengthen you, so that you should neither be afraid nor sad at my departure. I know full well that my words are speech and language which you now hear with your ears, for I am still talking to you. Nevertheless, they are far too deep for you, far beyond your comprehension. When you see me taken from you, the very words which I am now speaking and the very words of comfort I am now declaring will all too quickly pass out of your mind and be completely forgotten. But later, when the Comforter whom I promised comes to you, it will be none other than he himself who shall teach you finely and fully. Then will you understand everything, then be able to recall every word that ever I spoke to you. If this were not so, I would have spoken in vain, and you would have forgotten all I said. The reason for this is that these words of mine have not as yet penetrated the heart, and you have been unable to grasp their full meaning. You are but frail flesh and blood and only hear my words with your ears. That is why the Holy Ghost has to come, and write these words on your hearts. Then will you receive, and know that you possess the consolation I have given you.

[1] John 14:25–26.

An Ascension sermon

It is easy to repeat the words that our Lord Jesus Christ ascended into heaven and sits at the right hand of the Father. But the meaning of these words is not fully grasped until they are understood in the heart.

We must think of his lordship and his ascension as something active, ongoing, working, and must not let ourselves think that he is sitting up above, remote and isolated, while we are managing everything down here below. No! He ascended up thither for the simple reason that it is there that he can perform properly his real work, and from there exercise his lordship. Had he remained on earth in visible form before the people, he could not have wrought so effectually, for all the people could not have been with him and heard him all the time.

For this reason he inaugurated his ascension as an expediency which makes it possible for him to be in touch with all and to reign in all at one and the same time; to preach to all, and be heard by all, and to abide with all. Therefore, beware of imagining that he has gone, and is now remote and far from us. The opposite is true. It was while he was on earth that he was far from us; now he is most near.

Work

God works in us and we work together with him; through us he preaches, has pity on the poor, and comforts the broken-hearted . . . God himself milks the cows through him whose job it is to milk cows!

God does not consider how small or large the works are, but looks on the heart, which performs in faith and obedience to what its calling demands.

It is God's clear intention that all the saints[1] are to live in the same faith, and be moved and guided by the same Spirit; but in external matters to carry out different works.

No one is poor among Christians. If you do not have as much as the burgomaster, do you not rather have God the Creator of heaven and earth? And Christ? And prayer? The emperor does not have more! Remain in your station in life, be it high or low, and continue in your vocation.

Work, and let God give the fruits thereof!
Govern, and let him prosper your rule!
Battle, and let him yield the victory!
Preach, and let him make hearts devout!
Marry, and let him give you children!
Eat and drink, and let him give you health and strength!
Then it will follow, that whatever we do, he will effect everything through us. And to him alone shall be the glory!

[1] Christians (as Paul uses the word).

Joy in believing

Christ is a God of joy . . . A Christian should be and must be a man of joy.

The devil is the spirit of sadness, but God is the Spirit of joy, and he is our salvation.

We have more occasion for joy than sadness. The reason is we believe in the living God, and Christ lives, and we shall live also.

God can make himself known only through those works of his which he reveals in us, which we feel and experience within ourselves. When the experience is to learn that he is a God who looks into the depths and helps principally the poor, despised, afflicted, miserable, forsaken and those who are of no account, at that very moment a love for him is created and surges up from the heart's core. The heart overflows with gladness, and leaps and dances for the joy it has found in God.

In this experience the Holy Spirit is active, and has taught us in the flash of a moment the deep secret of joy.

You will have as much joy and laughter in life as you have faith in God.

Hope

Through hope we already dwell in heaven.

Our cause rests in the hands of him who distinctly tells us, 'No one can snatch them out of my hand.'[1] He said more: 'The gates of hell shall not prevail against my Church.'[2]

If we go under, then Christ, who is the almighty ruler of this world, must himself go under with us. Even if the cause of the Reformation were to collapse, I would much rather go to rack and ruin with Christ than stand triumphant with Caesar!

The one thing necessary is to believe, and to pray with complete confidence in the name of Christ, that God will give us the strength necessary. Without our help, counsel, thought or effort, he himself alone has brought forth his Kingdom, advanced it and preserved it to this day. I have not the slightest doubt that he will consummate it without our advice or assistance.[3]

God, in his gracious kindness, has given us in the vale of this world his holy, precious word, and his own dear Son . . . He will continue as God and Creator long after we are dead and gone. He was there before we appeared on the scene. To the end of time he will continue to gather to himself a little flock, and he will uphold it.

[1] John 10:28.
[2] Matthew 16:18.
[3] 2 Timothy 1:12; Ephesians 2:20.

Sources, suggested reading, and index

Sources, suggested reading, and index

The definitive edition of Luther's works is the *Weimarer Ausgabe*, some 100 volumes in all, begun in 1883 and not yet completed. It is normally quoted volume, page and line, thus: WA x.10.10. The letters are quoted WABr: again, volume, page, line, or number of letter; the Table Talk WATi: volume and number; the biblical prefaces WAB: volume, page, line.

Translations exist of major writings. See: *Library of Christian Classics*, vols. XV–XVIII, London 1955–68; *Luther's Works*, a 55-volume selection of Luther's main works, published in Philadelphia (1955), with subsequent reprints.

Atkinson, James, *Martin Luther and the Birth of Protestantism*. London 1968, 1981 (updated).

Bainton, Roland, *Here I Stand*. London 1950. Numerous reprints. (Strongly recommended.)

Rupp, E. G., *Luther Studies*. London 1953.

Todd, J. M., *Luther*. London 1982.

Watson, Philip, *Let God be God*. London 1947.

In the index which follows, the figure in bold type refers to a page of the present book. All references are to the *Weimarer Ausgabe*, volume, page, line.

3 vii.215.1–22; WABr v.405–7.

4 xl.1.33.7–11; lvi.158.10–14, 171.8–10, 247.15–17, 226.6–7.

5 xlvi.171.8–10; xl.1.47.28.

6 lvi.441.15–443.8; 446.11–16; xxxix.1.265ff.

7 vii.553.23–554.9; WAB vii.2–27; ii.98.18ff.

8 xl.2.37.26ff; v.396.13–397.9; ii.35.32ff; xii.338.

9 lvi.414.15, 17f; xli.190f; ii.113.5–8; xxv.368.2–40.

10 ii.113.36ff; x.2.322–6; WATi ii.1543, 1490; ii.3.111.35ff.

11 xxxiii.61f; ii.690.24f; xl.2.183.23; ii.51.15–24, 58.38ff.

12 v.176.29ff (441.15ff); xlvi.237.20–28; xviii.784.11f; ii.128.29–32.

13 xliii.458f; xlvi.237.21; i.138.13ff; i.614.17ff; xliii.393.9ff.

14 Letter to Wenzeslaus Link, 10 July 1518. WABr 184ff, 187.

15 iv.9.28; xl.1.46; xl.1.207.

16 xl.3.179f; i.350–65.

17 lvi.263.17ff; lvii.11.21ff.

18 WABr iv.271–3; x.1.(1).720.3ff; xlvi.658; WAB vii.19.6–7.

19 vii.570.30–571.13; x.1.(1).114.15–20.

20 WABr i.133–4.

21 xlvii.184; xxv.120; ii.95.16–18; WABr v.199–400; xxvi.172; WATi iv.4774.

22 vii.107.7–13.

23 80–130; vi.232.12–16; vii.232.22–44; WATi iii.2918.

24 vi.235.13–236.4; ii.127.3–27.

25 xxxv.213f (cf. WABr x.488).

26 liv.491.21–30.

27 ii.756.17ff; xxviii.580; xi.229f.

28 vii.683.8–26; vii.676; x.2.22f, 191; xv.78 et al; xxi.332f.

29 i.509–653; xxviii.208; xlv.621f.

30 vi.404–69; li.29ff; vi.407–8.

31 xlvi.184f, 186f; WATi i.181; li.239–40; xix.642, 643; li.246.

32 ii.252; xviii.389; WATi iv.4391; xxiii.404.5–7; WATi ii.2741(b); xxx.2.700–710(8).

33 ii.742–58; vi.532.5–18; xlix.74f; vi.24(13); i.286, 595.

34 vi.497–573, 363.1–19, 364.

35 ii.694.33–695.15; 742.

36 Catechism; ii.724–37; WATi i.522.

37 vi.353–78; ii.80–130; ii.111.35–114.4.

38 vi.353–78; vi.511.24–512.2; ii.742–58.

39 lii.208f; ii.753.17–24.

40 ii.748; lii.519f.

41 Heidelberg Disputation 1518. Theses xxi–xxv; i.350; xl.3.617.

42 Letter to a prior, 23 June 1516. WABr i.46–7.

43 Letter to Spenlein, 8 April 1516. WABr i.35–6.

44 Letter to a friar, WABr i.35–6.

45 Heidelberg Disputation 1518. Thesis xx; i.350ff.

46 xliv.73–4; xvii.2.203.

47 xl.1.78.6, 79.25; WATi 5658(a); xlvi.185.26ff.

48 WABr x.604–7; x.2.53–60; WABr vi.267.

49 xix.185–251; Worms (1521) ii.555; WABr i.220–22; ii.136–42.

50 lvi.325.2ff, 359.1ff, 356.4–7; WABr ii.140.13–22.

51 Letter to an Austrian nobleman, 1 September 1524. xviii.1–7.

52 vi.104–34; xv.516–33; ii.685–97; xxiii.714; WABr x.226–8.

53 x.1.(1).62ff.

54 xli.480; xvii.2.302; xxxii.253–5; ix.439–46.

55 lii.249f; xv.516–33.

56 xlv.614–15.

57 xii.562.12–565.29.

58 xliv.6; xi.258; xii.132f; xlix.609; xxxi.1.436f.

59 WATi ɪɪ.2342(a), 1822, 2153; WATi ɪ.676; WABr vɪɪ.66f; vɪɪ.548.4f; xʟ.3.196, 412; xxv.347.

60 ɪɪɪ.389.34; xxx.2.700–710.

LUTHER'S SEAL
(with a dove above his head)